HAGIOS PAULOS
Book 2

Stean Anthony

Yamaguchi Shoten, Kyoto

山口書店，京都

Hagios Paulos is Greek for Saint Paul

Hear my voice at:
<http://www35.tok2.com/home/stean2/>

Hagios Paulos Book Two
©2013 Stean Anthony
Author's profits
See end of book for details
PRINTED IN JAPAN

Doxa
To God only wise be glory
Through Jesus Christ
For ever, amen

Rom 16.27

Hagios Paulos 2
Contents

Preface		17
1.	Voice Rising	20
2.	True God	21
3.	Bless This SP	22
4.	What Was Needed	23
5.	Here We Are Now	24
6.	Go Forward Now	25
7.	What's the Message	26
8.	New Gospel	27
9.	Kletos	28
10.	Son	29
11.	Opinions Differ	30
12.	Liberation	31
13.	New Pagans	32
14.	Make Clear	33
15.	Barabba Barbaroi	34
16.	Not Blasphemy	35
17.	Resurrection 1	36
18.	Believe	37
19.	Paul Blesses	38
20.	Roman Church	39

21.	Eucharisto	40
22.	Thelema	41
23.	Longing to See You	42
24.	Charisma	43
25.	Harvest	44
26.	Pistis 1	45
27.	Hab 2.4	46
28.	Truth Known	47
29.	Ps 19.1	48
30.	Unlight	49
31.	Jer 10.1-10	50
32.	Used	51
33.	Happens in the Head 1	52
34.	Happens in the Head 2	53
35.	Happens in the Head 3	54
36.	Happens in the Head 4	55
37.	Happens in the Head 5	56
38.	Happens in the Head 6	57
39.	Wrath	58
40.	Eritheia	59
41.	Do Good	60
42.	Heaven Prize	61
43.	Helleni	62

44.	Grammata	63
45.	Father	64
46.	Mother	65
47.	Healer Be	66
48.	God Was Always There	67
49.	By Nature	68
50.	Polishing Ourselves	69
51.	Calling You	70
52.	Exemplars	71
53.	Peritome	72
54.	Because God	73
55.	Nefesh	74
56.	Greeks Are Jews	75
57.	Apollo	76
58.	End Time Thought	77
59.	Kaka Has Alpha	78
60.	Make It Better P	79
61.	Deep Need	80
62.	In Peace Let Us Pray	81
63.	Hilasterion	82
64.	Sin-Free	83
65.	Atonement	84
66.	Pistis 2	85

67.	Who Was It	86
68.	Patriarch	87
69.	Becoming a Jew	88
70.	Faith First	89
71.	Abraham 1	90
72.	Somewhat Obscure	91
73.	Paulsong: Daddy	92
74.	Faith Sufficient	93
75.	Abraham 2	94
76.	Resurrection by God	95
77.	Shield Away	96
78.	Paulsong: Forgiven	97
79.	Paulsong: In Our Weakness	98
80.	Revelation 1	99
81.	Revelation 2	100
82.	Retribution	101
83.	Can't Explain That	102
84.	Earth Nature	103
85.	Felix Plan	104
86.	How They Taught 1	105
87.	How They Taught 2	106
88.	Paulsong: Earth-foot Adam	107
89.	Thy Kingdom	108

90.	Adam's Sin	109
91.	Adam Sinless	110
92.	Confession	111
93.	Good in the End	112
94.	Lift Up Your Heads	113
95.	David	114
96.	Death Die	115
97.	Life Joy	116
98.	Freedom 1	117
99.	New Life	118
100.	With Him Rising	119
101.	He Lives He Lives	120
102.	Alive to God in Christ Jesus (XI)	121
103.	Where is God	122
104.	Not For Now	123
105.	Slaves to Life	124
106.	Freedom 2	125
107.	Christ Victory (XV)	126
108.	Soul-Fruit	127
109.	Marriage	128
110.	Evolved	129
111.	Whose Message	130
112.	Don't Touch	131

113.	Sold to Sin	132
114.	Ginosko	133
115.	Sin-Enslaved	134
116.	Where Turn	135
117.	Living In Me 1	136
118.	Living In Me 2	137
119.	Relief Deliver	138
120.	Rising Above	139
121.	Nomos Law	140
122.	Hamartia 1	141
123.	Hamartia 2	142
124.	Cut Free!	143
125.	Christ Heals	144
126.	What?	145
127.	Poles	146
128.	Paulprayer	147
129.	Shoutings Against 1	148
130.	Shoutings Against 2	149
131.	Shoutings Against 3	150
132.	Shoutings Against 4	151
133.	Song in Favor 1	152
134.	Song in Favor 2	153
135.	Song in Favor 3	154

136.	Greatest Love	155
137.	God is Spirit	156
138.	Eve	157
139.	Set Free	158
140.	Prison Break	159
141.	Flesh and Spirit	160
142.	Celibate Priest	161
143.	Sarx 1	162
144.	Sarx 2	163
145.	Sarx 3	164
146.	Paulbridge	165
147.	Diplomatic	166
148.	Abba	167
149.	Persecuted	168
150.	Apocalipsis	169
151.	Hope	170
152.	Patiently Waiting	171
153.	Intercedes	172
154.	Stenagmois 1	173
155.	Stenagmois 2	174
156.	Pneuma 1	175
157.	Forgiven	176
158.	Predestined	177

159.	Remembering	178
160.	All Given	179
161.	Unlock	180
162.	New Elect	181
163.	Not Cast Away	182
164.	Not Alone	183
165.	Not Abandoned	184
166.	Victory in His Love	185
167.	More Than Conqueror	186
168.	Christ in Command	187
169.	Hard to Say	188
170.	Eleous 1	189
171.	Imperative	190
172.	Sword	191
173.	Eleous 2	192
174.	Hosea 2.23	193
175.	Paul Then	194
176.	Paul Now	195
177.	Seized It	196
178.	Rock in Sion 1	197
179.	Rock in Sion 2	198
180.	Christos Telos	199
181.	Paul Is Lamb	200

182.	Father Will Love	201
183.	Upleap	202
184.	From Among	203
185.	Not Disappointed	204
186.	Onoma Kiriou	205
187.	Tell 'em	206
188.	Podes	207
189.	Me?	208
190.	Hurting	209
191.	Paul is a Jew	210
192.	Elijah	211
193.	Elect	212
194.	Bitter Speaking	213
195.	Apostle to the World	214
196.	Vitality	215
197.	Paulsong: Knead the Dough	216
198.	God-Rooted	217
199.	Pleroma Patch	218
200.	Tree Walking	219
201.	Way Digging	220
202.	Still and Good	221
203.	City of Peace	222
204.	Nous 1	223

205.	Nous 2	224
206.	Adelphoi	225
207.	Paulsong: Soma en Christo	226
208.	Paulsong: Agape Sincere	227
209.	Eulogeite!	228
210.	Irenically	229
211.	Bright Coals	230
212.	Crucified Us	231
213.	Angelic Authority	232
214.	Survive!	233
215.	Taxes and Debts	234
216.	Agapan Allelous	235
217.	Hopla tou Photos	236
218.	Beef and Oysters	237
219.	Party Today	238
220.	Snakes on Stakes	239
221.	To Whom	240
222.	Do Not Judge	241
223.	Do Not Despise	242
224.	Clear Up	243
225.	Not Octopi	244
226.	New Light	245
227.	Not Eating	246

228.	World Good	247
229.	Long-Termers	248
230.	Makarioi	249
231.	Give	250
232.	Read Scripture	251
233.	Harmony 1	252
234.	Accept One Another	253
235.	All Souls	254
236.	Teacher	255
237.	Priest	256
238.	Prison-life	257
239.	Task	258
240.	Name	259
241.	Paulsong: Paul Span	260
242.	Iberia	261
243.	NSEW	262
244.	Hispania	263
245.	Peril	264
246.	Blessing	265
247.	Future	266
248.	Vests West	267
249.	Vests East	268
250.	House-Builders Needed	269

251.	Paidagogos	270
252.	Scribe	271
253.	For God	272
254.	One His Master's Business	273
255.	Perfect Love	274
256.	Harmony 2	275
257.	Revealed	276
258.	Flashback	277
259.	Irreconcilable	278
260.	Paulsong: Anastanta	279
261.	Paulsong: Magdala Told Me	280
262.	Fuori le Mura	281
263.	The Way to Follow	282
264.	Farewell My Children	283
265.	Alpha Doxa	284
266.	Omega Doxa	285
267.	Saint Paul	286
	Greek Glossary	287
	Author's Profits	293
	Profile	294
	Prayer & Word of Blessing	295
	Books by Stean Anthony	296

Preface

This is Book Two in my series *Hagios Paulos* (Saint Paul in Greek).

The first book was a long narrative poem, intended to be a kind of pop-rock ballad, in which Saint Paul sings the story of his life.

This book is different in style, being a commentary and a response to Saint Paul's *Letter to the Romans*, and also including verses which represent what Saint Paul was thinking about in relation to the content of the letter and his own life (continuing from the earlier book).

There is a theme uniting this book with my earlier books. This is my belief that Saint Paul's message is not quite the same as it was 2,000 years ago.

The needs then and now are different. Then, he was walking away from Jerusalem. Now, let us walk towards Jerusalem, saying, "God is Love."

As I made the book, I realized that I was seeking to understand my own faith, and that struggle is found in this poetry.

Saint Paul's letters are full of bright jewel-phrases which encapsulate the truth, and my little poems are intended to do the same. You will find that many of the little poems are in fact quotations.

You will also find some verses which are pure fiction, and the point I am making is that even in fictional aspects you can find the deepest truths.

There is appended a glossary of Greek words which are important to Paul's message. I have included these because of their intrinsic interest.

Greek remains a foreign language to so many Christians, even though it is the primary language of their holiest book. With the tools on the internet, it is in fact quite easy to read the Bible in Greek.

001   Voice Rising

How the voice rose upwards
It was the sweetest fragrance of an Arabian tree
He was singing the letters of Saint Paul
I saw that strange man in my mind
Burnt black and beaten laughing he said follow.

pash

002   True God

Hear, O Israel, this song of God.
It is the one true God in all eternal time
In His beloved Christ this goodness
Asia and Egypt, listen, water of the sea!
Carry this love to the farthest sun-rising!

pash

003   **Bless This SP**

Blessed Saint Paul holy saint
Brightly your forehead gleams like a dome
Your dark eyes glimmer with joy
From your station close by His throne
Bless my little book that it serve God's love!

pash

004   What Was Needed

Taking an historical need
For an everlasting explanation?
In those years we were fighting ourselves
Everything we said was persuasion
Christ in glory bringing God to the world!

                                                                        pash

005   Here We Are Now

Take your chains off me you willful fools!
Greedy for your own self-interest
Serving the earth in yourself without heaven
God in Christ-cross bright in the skies
Break the mold to keep the goodness safe!

pash

006   Go Forward Now

You can't see it but I can see it
You can't hear it but I can hear it
You can't know it but I can know it
You won't act until the chance has gone
Today we must, not tomorrow, today!

						pash

007 What's the Message

The message was always the same.
How many times did you need to be told?
How many Loves existed?
The sun rose through endless space,
Vast time! Love was always and is real.

pash

008   New Gospel

Is this a new gospel that I am to tell you?
It is not! It is the obedience of the Christ
In accordance with the Eternal Will
To accomplish for the non-Jew, let me say the world,
The knowledge that salvation lives in God.

pash

009 Kletos

Paul, a servant of Jesus Christ
Called to be an apostle
Kept for this especial task.

Rom 1.1

010   Son

I am here to tell you about the Son of God
A holy name declaring unity with God
To bring you and all the world to salvation.

Rom 1.4

011 Opinions Differ

They won't accept this from me whatever I say.
How can I persuade them of this great truth?
The Lord guide me to show them that it's you.

pash

012   Liberation

Freed by our faith our mind filled with the love
Lived on earth by the Lord Jesus
Following that love without fear.

                                                    pash

013   New Pagans

They called us new pagans, Godless blasphemers
Worshipping a mortal – In part they were right
This was how the Father opened Heaven.

                                                                        pash

014   Make Clear

Men make distant by language and laws

The holy simplicity of God's beauty

Again and again we must pull off those dusty layers!

pash

015 Barabba Barbaroi

Shall we despise one another for lack of knowledge?
Shall I call you a Gentile, and you call me Barbarian?
God's love will take away such childish words.

pash

016   Not Blasphemy

It is not nonsense nor a blasphemy.
His proximity to God, an angel-phrase.
Son of God, a family-term in eternal truth.

Rom 1.4

017   Resurrection 1

Known to us through resurrection from the dead

Jesus Christ our Lord, this life-return and re-appearing

A curtain of heaven open on our souls.

Rom 1.4

018   Believe

**Given power by Him in His name to tell you
That if you believe and follow this truth
Everything for you will be better than before.**

Rom 1.5-6

019   Paul Blesses

A letter to the beloved of God in Rome

We are all called to be holy, grace to you!

Peace from God our Father and Lord Jesus Christ.

Rom 1.7

020   Roman Church

The Lord has told me in my own heart
And in the words of others your great goodness,
How the church grows with you, Praise God!

Rom 1.8

021   Eucharisto

First of all let me thank God.
I thank God by Jesus Christ
Your faith is spoken up so strong to all.

                                        Rom 1.8

022   Thelema

Help us Lord to follow thy will
Thy heaven-will be done on earth
May we prosper by thy will.

Rom 1.10

023   Longing to See You

To be with you again across this gulf
The wide seas and the constant winds
God might wing my spirit to be with you!

Rom 1.11

024   Charisma

To be with you to share with you

A spiritual gift together, to be strengthened

So that we might lift each other up higher in faith.

Rom 1.10-11

025   Harvest

Harvest will be great among you
Ignorant become wise
Slaves win new freedom and joy in Christ.

Rom 1.13-14

026   Pistis 1

The message is salvation for the one who believes.
First the Jew, and now the world to God.
Your soul will live in this true and perfect faith.

                              Rom 1.16-17

027   Hab 2.4

In the book that I have taught you
The true goodness of God is told
Through that goodness live by Christ in faith.

Rom 1.17

028   Truth Known

Wrath of God from heaven upon the wicked
The ones who suppress the truth I sing
God's truth is revealed, the scroll is in my hands.

Rom 1.18-19

029   Ps 19.1

The eternal power of God, His divine nature,
Not seen because too bright
Known in the making of all that is.

                                        Rom 1.20

030   Unlight

O I told you before again and again.
Childish unthinking ungrateful worms!
Your hearts grew dark with your denial of God.

Rom 1.21

031   Jer 10.1-10

Wisdom turned to folly
Trading the glory of the immortal One
For images of men, or birds, or snakes.

Rom 1.22-23

032 Used

In these pagan practices licentious
It is not God's will that these boys and girls
Against their will should serve this impure greed.

Rom 1.24-32

033   Happens in the Head 1

It's all inside your head, Paul, you're just a dreamer.
Possessed by empty dreams of folly.
Back to the book, Paul, stay with the truth!

                                              pash

034   Happens in the Head 2

Something so small like a fly's wing blurring
O I am a particle of dust in the storm
On the floor shaking when that time is past.

                                                                pash

035 Happens in the Head 3

Elated with power Christ liveth in me!
No doubt, no dark, no demons laughing
Later I'm praying as the flood waters rise.

pash

036 Happens in the Head 4

Returning again to the scene
Asking myself over and over again
Why didn't I understand what was going on?

                                                                pash

037   Happens in the Head 5

Call it negative nostalgia said the angel

To survive you must deny this, with all your strength

Live now love now say I love thee Christ!

pash

The phrase "negative nostalgia" came from a sermon by Pope Francis.

038   Happens in the Head 6

You want to hold that sin too much
Let it go, let that impulsion wither in the wind
The bright wind of God's Holy Spirit.

                                                                pash

039   Wrath

Man who has done iniquity
In despite of God's merciful goodness
Receive the wrath of God in judgment.

Rom 2.1-9

040   Eritheia

In the House how they seek to promote themselves

Going wrong again even as they try to be good

God sent us the true spirit which is selfless love.

                                                              pash

041   Do Good

For each according to the good they do
Her patience seeking honor and glory
Immortal she shall be in the gates of Heaven.

                                                            Rom 2.7

042   Heaven Prize

The good rewarded!
The Jew first and now you also.
God is truly just and fair.

Rom 2.10

043   Helleni

Glory and honor and peace
To those that do good to the Jews
To the Hellenes and for God.

Rom 2.10

044   Grammata

On the scroll the inky figures dance
Know the meaning, can I know the truth?
Dimly through this mirror the brightness glimpsed.

                                                              pash

045   Father

This was the truth I learnt at home.
My own father taught the holy words.
I have walked a long road for thee, O Christ!

                                        pash

046 Mother

God in our lives from the first light.
The brightness in the streets of Tarsus.
My mother singing as she made the broth.

pash

047   Healer Be

Hands of a healer   or   hands of a hurter
Priest of the Lord now and forever
Place your healing hands upon the world.

pash

048   God Was Always There

The Jew first and now you also!
There was goodness in you by God's grace
A natural goodness, loving kindness in your heart.

Rom 2.14-15

49 By Nature

If they do goodness (as we hold by the Book)
How shall we receive them? In a natural world
There is good, but not the holiness of heaven.

Rom 2.14

050   Polishing Ourselves

He was a gentle teacher as they told me
Inviting us to become better Jews than we were
To make the best words brighter in our lives.

pash

051   Calling You

Heaven's heat at the heart of the earth
In your hands the power
Pray up heaven and change this world.

                                                            pash

052   Exemplars

My sons in faith you must be what you say you are
Perfect teachers of what is perfectly good
Not in form or cloth only.

Rom 2.17-29

053 Peritome

Ancient sign of faith, the cutting round
The covering removed, the covenanted people
Not required of women, please note, because

Rom 2.5-29

054   Because God

Why then should we wish to become a Jew?
In this seal of circumcision, the promise of God
Nothing on earth has more value than that.

                                    Rom 3.1-2

055   Nefesh

Thou my soul my life that are beloved to God
Take thy feet out of the grave do not walk there
Leave that thought forever walk a sky-road now.

pash

056   Greeks Are Jews

What I am saying here is unthinkable for them
That your commitment to belief in God
By grace of Christ, this makes you Jew.

Rom 3.1-2

057 Apollo

In Greek filled with power His resurrected body
Wrestles with Apollo beautiful false angelos
Look how the truth fills the body with heaven light!

pash

058   End Time Thought

It was a crisis of universal time.
All wrong, nothing sufficient to appease the wrath.
In this pure sacrifice we could start again.

pash

059 Kaka Has Alpha

Just look what happened then and after.
Have you not known yet how the foe
Works for God in secret and open ways?

pash

060   Make It Better P

There is not one	there is one
Not one who understands	there is one
Not one who seeks God	there is one
All have gone astray	one stands firm
All alike are worthless	one worth every one
Not one does good	one did well
Not even one	there is one
Throats are open graves	one sings heaven
Deceiving tongues	one tells truth
Asp on lips	honey in one
Mouths cursing	one blessing
Quick to shed blood	quick in salvation
Ruin and misery	life jubilation
Way of peace not known	one peace giving
No respect for God	love of God singing.

Rom 3.10-18

061   Deep Need

Israel this was the burden of faith.
To feel that we were never right with God.
The gift in Jesus is to know that we are saved.

Rom 3.19-20

062   In Peace Let Us Pray

Grasp that God is first unutterable glory
Surpassing brightness
Purify yourself to join His sanctity.

pash

063   Hilasterion

In my grief I knew no limit and all the world was me
A mercy seat established in the heaven for my sin
Forgiven for what I'd done to him that day.

Rom 3.25

064   Sin-Free

It was a revelation to me that the unclean
And the clean should be equally in need
That by Christ both are equally forgiven.

Rom 3.22-26

065   Atonement

It was not thinkable for us despite Isaiah.

In this atonement therefore, this old way, this new way,

God's Love be given to the whole world.

Rom 3.25

066   Pistis 2

Not forgiven simply by the good deeds.

We hold that you are forgiven by your faith.

Embraced and healed by God, up to heaven by Christ.

Rom 3.28

067   Who Was It

There was a finger in the making of my letters
It was not me
Making the message less clear.

                                             Rom 4

068   Patriarch

Father Abraham just to say your name
The law the holy rules that made us.
I was so proud to be there with them.

                                    Rom 4.1

069   Becoming a Jew

What I am saying is that what was so good,
Especially to the ones from far away,
Being a Jew! That belief in God is a good.

Rom 4

070 Faith First

My dear Plato faith in God is all.
Of course you must do good
But the whole thing rests in the love of God.

Rom 4

071   Abraham 1

Father Abraham teaching us a beginning
From this point His purpose chose this people
From this point He gathers the whole world.

                                        Rom 4.10

072   Somewhat Obscure

Clarity lacking, or some part missing?

Those of the law inherit? Faith is worthless?

The new faith in Christ surpasses what we were told before.

Rom 4.14-15

073   **Paulsong**

Daddy Abraham you were Pops
We were sitting on your knee
All your children who love God
God the Father, One true God
Never again to hurt each other
Loving each other perfectly
Giving each other gifts of love
Do not look at what is different
Look only on heaven above
Count on the fingers the things we share
Start at the top – God loves us always
Right to the end – love one another
Paul today now sing this song!

                                                         Rom 4.16

074   Faith Sufficient

He believed in God and it was possible
He believed in God and He delivered
He believed in God and there's a miracle.

Rom 4.18-22

075   Abraham 2

The miracles of God teach us to follow.
Children born into faith when it cannot be.
A dead body cannot live, but life is restored.

Rom 4.19

076 Resurrection by God

We believe in God the Father
He raised the Lord Jesus to life from death
This was done to make the whole world a Jew.

Rom 4.24-25

077   Shield Away

Like a lamp guarded by an iron shield
How bright the light fills the house now
Revealed within us the light of God.

                                                                    pash

078   Paulsong

Forgiven by the faith we have
Through our Lord Jesus Christ
We have found peace with God
By this love we stand in grace.
We proclaim our hope in heaven-glory
We're proud of the suffering
We persevered growing stronger
Suffering taught us patience
Hope grew in us always
There was no disappointment
God's love through the Holy Spirit
Bright in our hearts.

Rom 5.1-5

079   Paulsong

In our weakness Christ died for us
When we were wrong and far from God.
To die for another, to teach by this gift
That God's unfailing love is greater than we.
While Adam in us sinned, Christ died.
The perfect one given by God, of sinless love
Forgiven by his sacrifice, his blood washed us.
I was a Greek and in this I am Jew,
In the life of Christ with God I now may live,
Even to rise to the eternal light of heaven.
Reconciled to God and saved, this is my song!

Rom 5.6-11

080   Revelation 1

Our nature explained by the fall in Adam
The truth of God as Moses taught not given,
Given we know, for God be thus, live well.

Rom 5.12

081   Revelation 2

Our nature godly when we follow His word
Their nature unclean? Love is a teacher
The beauty of God's secrets tell them all!

pash

082   Retribution

When I taught them I taught them this.
If you do wrong, if you disobey God's laws, if you sin,
God will certainly act, that moment or later, He will.

                              pash

083   Can't Explain That

This was what I saw in Jerusalem and the world

Clear as daylight to me then, but it is also clear now

That I know only this, God holds everything safe.

pash

084 Earth Nature

Well basically Adam is you, the name means earth
Don't do that, and he listened to her, and he did it,
But Abraham obeyed, even against all nature.

                                            pash

085   Felix Plan

But God was Himself in that disobedience

And in the obedience, disobeying in fact was obeying,

And to sacrifice your beloved son like that, what was that?

				pash

086   How They Taught 1

To bring salvation to the pagan world
God's Holy Word embodied as one man
A healer and teacher, Angelos-Apollon-Theos.

                                                              pash

087   How They Taught 2

The time was right to tell the deepest truth
Look Father Zeus will show you God Almighty
Look at Apollo beautiful Christ, look at Artemis.

pash

088   Paulsong

Earth-foot Adam knew by God
No book given till Uncle Moses
Didn't have a name for those naughty things
Not until the Book put the teaching on.

Death had a kingdom from Adam to Moses
Under Stonehenge the bones of sacrifice
Buried alive in the ancient swamps
When the king dies, let 'em go with him.

Leaping up from the death-bound earth
Christ the heaven-bird fiery phoenix
Holy unburning on his feathery back
The children soar to the big blue sky.

Rom 5.12-15

089   Thy Kingdom

Who shall reign – the primal teaching.
Who reigned from Adam to Moses?
Who is the King enthroned in Zion?

Rom 5.14

090   Adam's Sin

When we talk about Adam
And put the blame on him
We are talking about ourselves and what we did.

Rom 5.15

091   Adam Sinless

Adam was the figure of the Christ
In his creation made perfect man
The image of God free from sin unfallen.

                                                        pash

092   Confession

Proclaiming salvation in Christ Jesus
I confess that I spoke ill of my own people
Let me tell the love and goodness in the Jew!

pash

093   Good in the End

There's a beauty in this making all perfect

Humanity made sinners by Adam's disobedience

By the obedience of the later man that error was forgiven.

Rom 5.17

094   Lift Up Your Heads

If we remain in Adam with our feet in the mud
How shall we climb the path to the city
Through the gates, up the steps
And sit between the columns?

pash

095   David

David sings to us the same song
To choose wrong (which I call sin) is the path ending
To choose life is the path up to God.

                                                            pash

096   Death Die

Those wrong ways, all that does not lead to God,

Die in that so that death may die and then we rise

Baptized to new life in His resurrection.

pash

97 Life Joy

Life is the joy I have that God's love is with me
Death is the grief that I cannot find God
Christ clears the clouds of sin, we rise with Him!

                                                pash

98   Freedom 1

Our old self was crucified with Christ
The body ruled by sin has died
Slaves no more, we are set free from wrong.

Rom 6.6-7

99   New Life

We died with Christ to live

The bond slipped off and new yoke shouldered

Not breaking His word but born again, a robe of life.

Rom 6.8

100   With Him Rising

We died with Christ and we live with Christ
Risen from death we can die no more
Death has no power over Him.

Rom 6.8-9

101 He Lives He Lives

Death dies
Wrong ends forever
Life lives, it is life with God.

Rom 6.10

102   Alive to God in Christ Jesus (XI)

My children therefore offer your lives in goodness to God.

Do not follow that, do not serve that.

You are born again in grace,

Love is now the master.

Rom 6.11-14

103 Where is God

Those pagan temple practices of unrestrained libido
An obstacle for them, a cross for me
To live only in the flesh and for the flesh?

pash

104   Not For Now

The words were written to correct what was wrong.

The words remain but that time has gone.

God does not change but the world does change.

                                                    pash

105 Slaves to Life

To whom do we belong?
You were slaves to the wolf who devoured you
Slaves now to the new freedom Life!

Rom 6.16

106 Freedom 2

Freed from the wolf and serving God
Our lives became holy
We are rewarded with eternal life!

Rom 6.19-22

107 Christ Victory (XV)

    Wages of sin
Death | Eternal life
    Gift of God!

Rom 6.23

108   Soul-Fruit

The fruit of our new marriage

Through the death and resurrection our new vows

In our second marriage fruit for heaven.

Rom 7.1-6

109 Marriage

As a people we are married to God
In the contract we agreed to do many things
A good husband He supports us and protects us.

Rom 7.2

110 Evolved

Out of the darkness of the earth
Moses drew us into light
The laws taught us, the customs made us men.

Rom 7.7

111 Whose Message

Don't do that tells us what to do.
Who is speaking to me now?
Is that you Lord Jesus?

Rom 7.7-11

112 Don't Touch

How can the laws given to us by God

Lead to evil – Good is not always good

Laws on impurity, can't you see where that leads?

Rom 7.13

113 Sold to Sin

Sold into slavery lit. and fig.
The ones who heard my song in Corinth
Serving those masters in profane flesh.

Rom 7.14

114   Ginosko

To know deeply to know fully
In the earth to know by the flesh
In heaven the highest perfection known.

Rom 7.15

115 Sin-Enslaved

Sold as a slave!
What I want to do I do not do.
What I hate I do.

Rom 7.14-15

116 Where Turn

I know that Moses is good.
I do not do the good I want to do.
Is this darkness living in me?

Rom 7.16-17

117   Living In Me 1

I am not the one, it was death living in me.
It was not me, but it was Christ living in me.
Lord, I wrestle with my madness, help me win.

Rom 7.17

118 Living In Me 2

Bless God through Jesus Christ Our Lord.
Thanks be to God!
Salvation is Messiah.

Rom 7.25

119   Relief Deliver

My heart at war with myself every day.
To follow God or to fail to follow.
From the madness Jesus rescues me!

Rom 7.21-25

120   Rising Above

This is the new freedom, to be more perfect.
The grace of the Lord Jesus Christ given.
We win the fight and leave the earth below.

Rom 7.1-25

121 Nomos Law

That which is handed down in holy instruction
Law's a bad translation, let me say Moses
Holy commandments, life-teaching, all of scripture.

pash

122   Hamartia 1

Depriving yourself of God
Darkness is what this is
Hurting other people not loving Christ.

pash

123   Hamartia 2

This is where we must increase our strength.
Not ruled by fear of wrong, not living selfishly
But giving more love and glad in the good we do!

                                        pash

124   Cut Free!

You find me talking a lot about sin
Those inherited things which take us from God
Those unspeakable things which do not give life.

                                                                pash

125   Christ Heals

Dear children do not misunderstand me.
I am hinting of the grief in the flesh I knew,
Mind tormented over and over, but Christ heals me!

pash

126   What?

You may ask me why I do not write clearly

And why the substance is obscure and veiled

And you must remember the peril in which we lived.

                                                              pash

127 Poles

Two poles to make all clear to you
Earth on the left hand, Heaven on the right
By Christ who made all good choose right!

pash

128   Paulprayer

Eucharisto to Theo

Dia Iesou Christou tou kiriou hemon, amen.

Thanks be to God through Jesus Christ our Lord.

Rom 7.25

129   Shoutings Against 1

Abomination! No! Again, No!
That man you say is the promised one?
Your folly leads you to death!

Rom 8.1

130 Shoutings Against 2

Get him out of the holy precinct!
He will destroy us all!
The wrath of God will fall from heaven!

                                    Rom 8.1

131   Shoutings Against 3

You do not understand the Holy Text!
You do not read the signs correctly!
You have no learning and you have no right!

Rom 8.1

132 Shoutings Against 4

You're so certain God has chosen you.
So many like you led by darkness.
You'll destroy yourself and all you deceive.

Rom 8.31

133   Song in Favor 1

I am convinced above everything else I know
That God's love through Christ Jesus
Will hold me and save me no matter what.

Rom 8.39

134   Song in Favor 2

Where does my confidence come from?

From Christ Jesus by the will of God

Who revealed himself to me directly as I know and live.

                                                                        pash

135   Song in Favor 3

Through this Lord, God's own gift, to open heaven

To the Greek and Roman – you do not look at the Love

You do not see that this is how Jerusalem shall live!

pash

136   Greatest Love

God sent his own son in the weakness of man's flesh.

He was an offering for sin, so bad became good.

Now His Spirit lives in us by Christ.

Rom 8.3-4

137 God is Spirit

If you live according to the sinful nature you will die.
If Christ is in your heart the Spirit gives life
He raised Christ he will raise you to heaven.

Rom 8.9-13

138 Eve

Woman your earth sin painted the doorway.
Flesh in the mind taking God from me.
Jesus far greater than I was for thee.

pash

139   Set Free

The sexual thing between us far from home

The Greek wine, the laughter, their easy ways

But I must say no it is Christ who walks beside me.

					pash

140 Prison Break

Paul given Christ-will to break the fetters

Chains of lust in mind, chains of life on my children,

Prisoned-thought I'll break the walls for heaven!

                                                         pash

141   Flesh and Spirit

The putrid meat and bones is hung to the wind
God's holy resurrection promise to all people
We rise as angel spirits made of pure light.

                                                      pash

142   Celibate Priest

The rabbi had to be celibate
His sexual allure, his gifts, the power
No other way to keep him safe for God.

                                        pash

143   Sarx 1

Cultural difference. In my mission to them
I saw how their way was enslaved to flesh,
For my life with them what a thorn this was.

pash

144 Sarx 2

What has changed after so many years?
How they loved the human form (too beautiful)
Michelangelo? Was that for God? Flesh! Flesh!

pash

145 Sarx 3

Back to the beginning, the aroma pleased God
The best bits, you may eat the offering, in Rome
They understood this, eating Christ we become.

Jn 6.56

146   Paulbridge

Stand back a long way back and look

Everything is a bridge to bring God to everyone

That explains it, so the Love is given and better in that way.

pash

147 Diplomatic

Phrases to smooth the way

Mind of the flesh or mind of the spirit?

Choose that earthly creed or the breath of heaven.

pash

148   Abba

Led by the Spirit of God
We are the children of God
The Spirit gives us courage and we cry, Abba!

Rom 8.14-15

149   Persecuted

We suffer with Christ! The persecution of those years!
Just to survive, to hold on, to live through
Confident in His love and Heaven's glory.

Rom 8.17

150 Apocalipsis

All creation upon the cross
The glory is about to be revealed
Groaning in labor for the new world and heaven.

Rom 8.18-23

151   Hope

We hope for what we do not see
For hoping in the world before us
These pictures, these shapes, this is not hope.

Rom 8.24

152 Patiently Waiting

Do we place our hope in what we look upon?
Those false things I do not want to say them.
We hope in the unseen, which is the Eternal Father!

Rom 8.24-25

153 Intercedes

Who is the Spirit that intercedes for us
In the Doxa that is higher than everything
Who visits our hearts with mercy in this life?

Rom 8.26-34

154   Stenagmois 1

We do not know how to pray

The Spirit helps us in our weakness

The Spirit breathes within us deeper than ourselves!

                                                          Rom 8.26

155   Stenagmois 2

We do not know how to pray

The Spirit from above within our heart

Sorry to be for failing thee my own Christ with God!

Rom 8.26

156 Pneuma 1

The One who searches the heart
His Spirit is Himself there our helper always
Pleading for our souls before the eternal throne.

                                                Rom 8.27

157 Forgiven

For those who truly love God what shall there be?
My soul you are forgiven and accepted
You loved the Lord, be strong in that!

Rom 8.28-30

158 Predestined

Called and predestined and forgiven
Every soul is in the hands of God
A life to live, how shall we choose to be?

Rom 8.28-30

159 Remembering

Not for one moment did I ever forget
The hope that led me south to God's house
The voice of the martyr as he spoke Thy name.

Rom 8.28-30

160 All Given

If God is for us, who is against us?
He gave his own Son for each one of us
Through Him he gives us all that may be!

Rom 8.31-32

161 Unlock

If God is with us, who can be against us?
Find Him where I quote this
A key to the gates of heaven.

Rom 8.31, Ps 27.1–3, 118.6.

162 New Elect

Israel the elect, those loved by God
Jesus at the right hand of God
Greek and Roman, Briton, all go through!

Rom 8.33-34

163 Not Cast Away

Who can separate me from His love?
Neither the weariness and chains
Neither the loneliness and grief.

Rom 8.35

164　Not Alone

Who can separate me from His love?
Neither the long road and trouble
Neither the cold prison floor.

Rom 8.35

165 Not Abandoned

Who can separate me from His love?
Neither the bitter phrase
Neither the cross, nor the sword.

Rom 8.35

166 Victory in His Love

Nor height, nor depth
Nor anything in all creation
Can separate me from the love of God in Christ!

Rom 8.36-39

167 More Than Conqueror

Nor death, nor life, nor angels
Nor things now, nor things to come, nothing
Can separate me from the love of God in Christ!

Rom 8.36-39

168   Christ in Command

Almost I might forgo my own salvation
To give my own people the truth I know
Jesus of Nazareth the Messiah.

Rom 9.1-5

169 Hard to Say

The difficulty I had to say this
Not by race nor inheritance or tribe
But by grace through faith to be a new Israel.

Rom 9.6-14

170   Eleous 1

All is in the mercy of God
Those who choose Him as He chooses us
To belong to God and live in his mercy!

Rom 9.6-14

171   Imperative

Clear as day to us now

The holiness of God must be given to the world

This is God's work through Christ, not the will of man.

Rom 9.16-18

172   Sword

Our own people put us to death

Then the Romans

So many, so hard and yet we grew.

pash

173   Eleous 2

Vessels that might carry fire?
Vessels to be filled with mercy
Called for this from the Jew and the Gentile.

Rom 9.23-24

174   Hosea 2.23

Pity upon all the people
Choosing the one not chosen
They will say **Our God.**

Rom 9.25

175 Paul Then

The children of Israel are like sand of the sea
But only one part will be saved
That part is this church.

Rom 9.27-29

176 Paul Now

The children of Israel are like sand of the sea
Thousands of years like sand have run
A vast horizonless sea of souls in heaven!

Rom 9.27-29

177 Seized It

Freedom to walk in the light
Believing only in the love of Christ
They grasped it with both hands.

Rom 9.30

178 Rock in Sion 1

Greeks who love God are saved

Jews who do the rules without love are lost

Love of God is the foundation rock.

Rom 9.30-33

179   Rock in Sion 2

Petran Skandalou Rock of Offence.
Know that the shame is the glory!
Peter, thou and I, what was yours?

                                                        Rom 9.33

180 Christos Telos

They can be righteous and good

Doing all that we were taught

But Christ is the point to which the Book is leading.

Rom 10.4

181 Paul Is Lamb

Israel not Israel
Plenty of them, and they reject me
I will not say they shall not be saved by God.

Rom 10.1-4

(*Hagios Paulos Book One* p. 213)   Peace with Islam!   الله

182 Father Will Love

Who will ascend to heaven to bring Christ?
Who will descend to the depths to raise Christ?
God has done this for us, do you still not know?

Rom 10.6-7

183   Upleap

Say the words aloud for everyone to hear
Know without fear the truth in the heart
Believe that the true Messiah is Jesus Christ.

Rom 10.8-9

184   From Among

He died and came back to life you say?
This is known among the Greek gods.
This was the gift of the one true One.

Rom 10.9

185 Not Disappointed

Shall not be ashamed? My ironic voice
Phrases lost when they gathered fragments
The opposite true sometimes, to make a point.

Rom 10.11

186   Onoma Kiriou

No difference between Greek or Jew.
The same Lord is rich in love to all.
All who call on His name will be saved.

Rom 10.12-13

187   Tell 'em

How can they pray without belief?

How can they believe without being told?

How can they be told unless I send someone there!

Rom 10.14-15

188   Podes

How beautiful are the feet of those who bring good news.

It was our task to tell them of the love the prophet sang.

An ancient command to Israel which we obeyed.

Rom 10.15

189 Me?

I held out my hands
You ignorant stupid and dull clot-head
I held out my hands to you from day one!

Rom 10.21

190 Hurting

Hurting always that I had to say goodbye
Hurting always that they would not listen
Hurting always that they went so far as that.

pash

191   Paul is a Jew

A descendant of Abraham
From the tribe of Benjamin
I am a Jew myself and happy.

                                                                    pash

192 Elijah

Elijah appealed to God against them
(This is myself and it was also Him)
Elijah your fire you gave me.

pash

193   Elect

The remnant chosen by grace, these are the Jews
The ones who knew and believed in Him
This is the core of the new life today.

pash

194   Bitter Speaking

Our people who do not accept Salvation
In the bitterness of our martyrdom
We call them grave dwellers and dead prayers.

pash

195 Apostle to the World

I am speaking to the non-Jew which may seem today
Something utterly given but it was not
I stepped out into air and angels held me.

pash

196 Vitality

Their rejection of Him and his death
The death of others and my life
Spirit through the mind
All-heal
Life to the dead world!

pash

197   Paulsong

Knead the dough with flour and water
Knead the dough
Fold your hands about the rice ball
Fold your hands
Roll the dough Paul roll the dough
Fold your hands Paul pray the words
Roll the world Paul roll the bread roll
Roll the round along the skyway
Paul you're rolling on a heaven runnel
Knead the dough with flour and water
Paul arising in a holy strolling
Jesus rolling on the western road
Knead that dough Paul knead that dough!

                                                    pash

198 God-Rooted

Root of the olive reaches for God
Swim in the sweet oil back to God
Into the good earth deep to the heart.

Rom 11.16

199   Pleroma Patch

New onto Old to patch it up?
No, it won't work, the cloth will tear.
Pour Rome in a new amphora fill full Paul

                                                                Rom 11

200   Tree Walking

**Grafted on the tree from Greek and Rome
How beautiful in pagan is the name of God!
Gaul follows, Celtic, Saxon, Gott!**

pash

201 Way Digging

Back to the root
Root in the truth
Dig to the centre

root in deep nature
God who is love
gold words there.

pash

202   Still and Good

In the quiet inside the Lord sits waiting
Sing your love to the grieving cosmos
The Lord stands up now walk with Him Paul.

                                        pash

203   City of Peace

My dear brother and sister, Paul in the city!
But you know that city is the always-heaven
The deepest love is hand in hand with you.

                                                            pash

204   Nous 1

Who has known the mind of the Lord?

Who could be his counselor

Who could give to God that God should repay?

pash

205 Nous 2

The depth of the riches
Of the wisdom and knowledge of God!
Unsearchable are His judgments!

pash

206 Adelphoi

Brothers and sisters we are a living sacrifice
We must be holy and acceptable to God
Spiritual worship not conformed to the world
Transformed day by day in the knowledge of Christ
Our lives in service of God's love
Know His will
Be good and perfect as God wills.

Rom 12.1-2

207 Soma en Christo

Let us think of ourselves as we are.
There is a task for each of us.
In Christ all have their part to play
As we are all part of the same body
Limbs, and flesh, bones and blood!
Some shall prophesy, let them sing
Some shall serve others, let them serve
Some shall teach, let them teach
Some shall lift up, let them encourage
Some shall be generous, let them give
Some shall be leaders, let them lead
Some shall show mercy, let them do so with joy
Some shall be all this, let them be Love.

Rom 12.3-8

208   Agape Sincere

Love must be true let us hate what's bad
Hold to the good and love each other
Honor each other above ourselves
Serving the Lord with a bright faith
Joyful in hope
Patient in suffering
Constant in prayer.

Rom 12.9-12

209 Eulogeite!

Bless those who persecute you
Bless and do not curse
Rejoice with the joyful
Mourn with the sad
Live in harmony with one another
Do not be proud
Be loving to the lowly ones
Do not think yourself so great.

Rom 12.14-16

210   Irenically

For the wrong you suffer do not seek revenge
Do what is good in the eyes of all
Live at peace with everyone.

Rom 12.17-18

211 Bright Coals

When someone is hungry, feed them.
When they are thirsty, give them to drink.
On a cold day shovel the coal, hearth of love.

Rom 12.20-21

212   Crucified Us

Obey the authorities who govern
God gave them that power
Resisting them you may be resisting God
There will be judgment upon you
You must not obey those authorities over you
Are you so faithless and dull-spirited?
Obey in a shell of empty obedience
Resist them all the way to heaven
Trample upon their wicked authority
For they do not and will not refrain themselves
From instruments they have no right to use.

Rom 13.1-7

213 Angelic Authority

Submit to the governing authorities
The established powers not of this world
The holy ones instituted by God
The ministers of God through the silent air
In God's love growing, angels attend upon you.

Rom 13.1

214 Survive!

Pay what is due to them, pay the taxes
Give respect and honor to them   my children
Survive! You must do what you have to do.

Rom 13.7

215 Taxes and Debts

Pay your taxes and clear your debts
Cancel the sins you have listed up
Love for God and neighbor, this pays all.

Rom 13.8

216   Agapan Allelous

What debts might you have except that ye love one another?

As he told us, love is the sum of all He taught us

All prophets, all laws

Love one another as He loves us.

Rom 13.8-10

217 Hopla tou Photos

Now is the time to wake from sleep
Salvation is close at hand
The night is almost over and day is near
Let us fling away the robes of darkness
And put on the armor of light
Living in the daylight
Putting upon ourselves the Lord Jesus Christ
His spirit now within us bright and strong.

Rom 13.11-14

218   Beef and Oysters

Here is a friend who will not eat oysters
Here is a friend who will not eat beef
John in the wilderness lived on locusts in honey.

Rom 14.1-6

219 Party Today

Here is a friend who parties on Monday

Here is a friend who parties on Friday

John in the wilderness partied each day with God.

Rom 14.5-6

220 Snakes on Stakes

Eat the day to the Lord in thanks!
When you are hungry even pickled adders
Give thee strength to praise the Lord.

Rom 14.5-6

221　To Whom

Our lives are not our own, they belong to Christ.
He rose from death to be the Lord of all.
We live and die and rise to life in Him.

Rom 14.7-9

222   Do Not Judge

Why do you pass judgment on your brother or sister?
Why do you despise your brother or sister?
We will all stand before the judgment seat of God.

Rom 14.10

223 Do Not Despise

We live in a world of allegiance.
Do not despise them for their faith.
It is God who decides how everything shall be.

Rom 14.10-12

224 Clear Up

Let us refrain from judgment of each other
Neither stringing up the trip-wires to hurt them
Rather let us clear the ground of old explosives.

Rom 14.13

225 Not Octopi

Obvious to us then but not today
That every meal we take is a prayer to God
A poetry of repast, clean orisons not octopi.

Rom 14.14-23

226 New Light

Time in the hands of the Lord Jesus Christ
We walk in a new light – Food and drink
History and language are nothing to His Love.

Rom 14.14-23

227 Not Eating

Eating is not eating it is life to God
It is prayer and thought
It is reading and understanding of the Word.

Rom 14.14-23

228 World Good

Righteous life and peace and love
God's power in the far away Houses
Build each other – make the world good.

Rom 14.19

229   Long-Termers

We live in an old people's home
In a hospital world medicines are everywhere
Eat less, avoid harm, eat   God is Love.

Rom 14.14-23

230 Makarioi

Blessed in your confidence in Christ

Blessed in your trust in Jesus

Blessed in your sharing with brothers and sisters.

Rom 14.22

231 Give

Give strength to the weak, show your love
Build up your neighbor, show your love
When they insult you, respond with love.

Rom 15.1

232 Read Scripture

My children you must learn to read
The best among and the least among you
I am risen in the Word even to heaven height.

Rom 15.4

233   Harmony 1

Eternal God grant that you live in harmony
In accordance with the love of Jesus Christ
One voice to glorify God the Father.

Rom 15.5

234 Accept One Another

Why do I have to say again
Welcome one another as one family
Jew and non-Jew – will your folly never end?

Rom 15.7-8

235 All Souls

Long ago I met the Lord
I read those holy verses
Nations and peoples, heaven for every soul.

Rom 15.9-11 & Ps 18.49 & Deut 32.43 & Is 52.15

236   Teacher

As from my youth intended to be a teacher
By Christ all changed in me
I sing the good news that God loves the world.

Rom 15.14-16

237 Priest

Called to be a priest by God through Christ
I glory in Christ Jesus serving God
Speak to the non-Jew the holiest truths.

Rom 15.16-17

238   Prison-life

So many years under this arrest am I cursed
In kindness they let me meet and write
Visitors came, Christ-rising, task I am blessed.

pash

239   Task

Boast I shall about this task
By the Holy Spirit in me
Signs and wonders go upon the seas.

Rom 15.17-19

240 Name

Paul my name a secret sign among us
Like a wind in the sail on a fine day
The boat of the church visits every coast.

Rom 15.20

241   Paul Span

Song for the future song for today
Is there no more work for me now
Shall my life in Christ be over yet?

Did the Roman sword fall on me
Did I smash the stony paving
Brothers and sisters gifted in miracle.

Strange things saved us again and again
Some on a boat went to friends in Spain
Early days our love was strong!

> Rom 15.23-24

242   Iberia

Under my name the church fled Diocletian
Grandchildren of my children speaking Latin
Former slaves and sons of Rome to Spain.

pash

243 NSEW

Out of our poverty love to Jerusalem
From the north to our home in the south
From the south to our home in the north.

Rom 15.25-26

244 Hispania

When we have taken Rome to Jerusalem
Brothers and sisters pray for me
Wing to the Spanish and their children.

Rom 15.28-29

245   Peril

Pray for me that I may be safe
The old family still seek my life
Pray that our gifts may give strength to Love.

Rom 15.30

246   Blessing

By God's will may I come to you
With joy to be renewed together
God who gives peace be with you all, Amen.

Rom 15.32-33

247 Future

Minister in the church, I commend Sister Phoebe
Welcome her in the Lord as one of the saints
Help her in everything, she holds the future.

Rom 16

248   Vests West

Paul, cut that chatter making Mary minister
Such silly saying an anathema to me
Twelve were men
You want to put a woman on the tree?

pash

249 Vests East

Paul, finally, has your brain caught fire?
Gender is God-given
How can he or she
Be joined together in holy matrimony?

                                                                pash

250   House-Builders Needed

Loving souls together living love forever
Fleshly matters are a trivial thing
Happiness building love and strength I see.

pash

251   Paidagogos

Greet all the Church members too many to name
Especially those slaves in the grand estate
Those teaching Greek to the boys.

                                                    Rom 16

252 Scribe

To Marcellus the scribe my greetings
Copy the letters and keep them safe
Also those Testaments now arriving.

Rom 16

253   For God

O my family the grief I had to bear
Never wanted to say goodbye
God graffitied on the prison walls.

					pash

254 On His Master's Business

Greet the newly arrived with gifts of love

Seek out any from Alex or Cyrene

Seek out those with duty to trade and travel.

Rom 16

255   Perfect Love

My regret only that I cannot be with you

I long to teach ye about the perfection of God

Jesus Christ for you each one, a gift of perfect love.

pash

256   Harmony 2

Let there be love and agreement between you
No smooth-talk and false-speaking
Be wise in goodness and without guile or deceit.

pash

257 Revealed

Revelation of the mystery kept secret for so long

Spoken by the Prophets and declared to the nations

Through Jesus Christ to whom be glory forever, amen.

                                                                    pash

258   Flashback

Close your eyes Paul and you're there again
Fear has gone and joy remains, living again
Under the sun an everlasting voice of love.

                                        pash

259   Irreconcilable

My life from the death of Stephen
Our love oppressed by this utter hostility
The old family were lions, and we flew to live.

                                                    pash

260 Anastanta

Years ago and later in my gift of heaven

I knew that the cross of shame was glory

He held his arms outstretched in blessing

Hovering in the heavens a glory sign

Death was defeated by my sky-soarer

Under these wings the gift of life

Heavenly Father I thank you for your love

This fearful wonder of surpassing power

My hand holds His light-robe and I rise with Him!

pash

261 Magdala Told Me

The miracle of his warm presence
I recognized him by his smell
Before I saw him, I dared to hope it was Him.

Peter Told Me
Suddenly he was there with us standing there
The moment that our prayer achieved heaven
Walking toward us turning the storm to calm.

Thomas Told Me
Eternal Love taught us that day and forever
Body came to warm life, this is the resurrection
God said now the world may enter my holy Love.

Mary Told Me
Paul for the future the message is healing
The world is Jerusalem, in a prayer of love
Let the children stand together and pray!

262 Fuori le Mura

Stretched my body on his holy tomb
In a dream I learn the dream for real
Beat the sound and bring to heaven.

                                        pash

263   The Way to Follow

On the cold stone kneeling with a bowl
Serva had been on the streets selling
Paul washed her feet and kissed them.

                              pash

264   Farewell My Children

Time so short, the being together gone so soon
Those few words we spoke together
Etched in the air forever our love remains.

pash

Alpha   Doxa

Glory beyond the power of speech
Opinion in time rooted deep
Divinity unutterable, praise His brightness.

                                        pash

Omega   Doxa

**From Him and through Him
All things exist
Glory to God forever, amen.**

Rom 11.36

Saint Paul

I looked behind me
And there he was,
Dark, quite short in stature,
Fierce eyes and a disarming smile.
Paul, how shall we go forward?
He said, things always change,
But it was always the women first.
We talked to them in gatherings
In Asia and they were so glad,
The Holy Spirit, not our strength,
But God Himself through us,
And then they told others
And this new power changed us –
Jesus Christ, radiant upon us from heaven.
I'd say one bread, share with me,
Thank God, this bread, it's Love.

(reprinted from *Saint Mary 100* by Stean Anthony p. 117)

Greek Glossary

Abba:	(Aramaic) father (Greek) pater
Adelphos:	brother, member of the community
Agapao:	to love, in faith to follow God's will in action, a self-defining word for the new Church
Agathos:	intrinsically good, good in nature, profitable for goodness
Aion:	age, knowledge of God revealed in time for all time, eis tous aionas ton aionon (Rev 1.6)
Akeraios:	innocent, lit. unmingled, i.e. without bad motives. Be innocent as doves (Mt 10.16)
Aletheia:	truth, as opposed to falsity, sincerity, truth an attribute of God
Anastasis:	resurrection, lit. "stand up again," Christ rises from the dead, resurrection at the end of the age
Aphthartos:	incorruptible, immortal, undecaying, the glory of the immortal God (Rom 1.23)
Apokalipsis:	uncovering, revelation, salvation by God through Christ revealed for all people (1 Cor 2.10)
Apolitrosis:	redemption, release on payment of ransom, met. for atonement of sin by Christ (Rom 3.24)
Apologia:	speech in defense, defending the new understanding, Paul's task (Ph 1.16)

Barbaros:	foreigner who does not speak Greek, uncivilized, uncultured (LXX 2 Maccabees 2.21)
Chairo:	rejoice, also salutation, Chaire! Hail! (Lk 1.28)
Charis:	grace, favor, a special gift from God
Chrestos:	serviceable, pleasant, good, kind. My yoke is easy and my burden is light (Mt 11.30)
Chrestotes:	goodness, benignity, kindness, word favored in Romans, the kindness of God (Rom 2.4)
Chronos:	time in general (Jn 7.33 & Acts 1.6-7)
Dikaioo:	declare righteous, often translated as justify (a legal term) the acquittal of sin by God
Dinamis:	power, might, ability, wonderful works. The healing power of God in Christ (Mk 5.30)
Doulos:	bondslave, term of dignity in service of Christ. Mary describes herself as doule (Lk 1.38)
Doxa:	glory, God's (unutterable) splendor (root word is opinion) Sept. trans. Heb: Kabōd (Eze 1.28)
Egeiro:	to awaken, lift, raise up used lit. and metaphoric. in central concept of raising from death
Eirene:	peace, political peace, word of greeting, assurance of salvation, state of bliss (Rom 5.1)
Elaia:	olive tree (Latin: oliva Heb. zayith) fig. for prosperity (Rom 11.24)
Eleeo:	to have mercy on, Eleeson hemas, have mercy on us (Mt 9.27)

Eleutheroo:	to set free from bondage, to set free from sin (Jn 8.32-36)
Elpis:	hope in good, expectation of salvation, vital phrases used by Paul with the word hope
Epangelia:	promise, the promises of God, salvation through Christ (Rom 4.14)
Epikaleo:	to call upon by name, to appeal, to give a name, used in Acts (Acts 2.21)
Ergon:	work, deed, in the phrase "works of the law" the fulfillment of various Levitical prescriptions
Eritheia:	selfish ambition, factionalism, strife (Phil 2.3)
Ethnos:	race, nation, gentiles (Heb goiim)
Euangelion:	glad tidings from God about salvation through Christ, Gospel of the Kingdom (1 Cor 15.1-10)
Eucharisteo:	give thanks (Lk 22.17 & 22.19 & Rom 7.25)
Ge:	arable land, earth, main land, a region (Mt 6.19)
Gnosis:	intelligence, knowledge, perception of God's reality, knowledge of salvation (2 Cor 4.6)
Hagios:	holy, place set apart for God, saint (Lk 1.35)
Hidor:	water (Heb mayim) (Jn 1.26)
Hilasterion:	expiation, covering of the ark of the covenant, fig. for Christ (Rom 3.25 & Heb 9.5)
Hipsistos:	Most High, a title for God (Heb Eliōn) (Lk 1.35)
Horaios:	beautiful, blooming (Song 1.16 & Rom 10.15)

Huios:	son, descendant, one who follows another. "Son of man" OT periphrasis for man denoting weakness, Jesus's Messianic title for himself
Kairos:	time, a specific time, a period of time, at the appointed time (Mt 13.30)
Kaleo:	call aloud, invite, summon, name. To call to vocation, to call to redemption (Mt 4.21)
Kalos:	good which is beautiful, best, also adv well, good aimed at heaven. I am the good shepherd (Jn 10.11)
Karpos:	fruit, harvest, children, good results. Blessed is the fruit of your womb (Lk 1.42)
Katallasso:	reconcile, receive into favor of God (2 Cor 5.18)
Kirios:	master, lord, sovereign, title of respect for God, for the Messiah, LXX trans of Yhvh (Mk 12.29)
Kletos:	called, invited to a banquet, as apostle (Rom 1.1)
Ktisis:	creature, the act of creating, creation (Rom 8.21)
Martis:	witness for the Gospel, martyr (Acts 22.20)
Mello:	will, intend, to be about to do something, things which are sure to happen (Mt 16.27)
Nai:	yes, certainly, emphatic particle (Mt 9.28)
Nefesh:	soul, life, mind (Heb) see psiche.
Nomos:	Torah, divine instruction moral and sacred, Mosaic Law, scriptures in general (Rom 10.4)

Onoma:	name, identity, reputation, reality of God, bless the name of God (Ps 103.1 & Lk 11.2)
Ontos:	indeed, certainly, of a truth. Truly he was an innocent man (Lk 23.47)
Opheilema:	debt, that which is owed, sin (Mt 6.12)
Ophthalmos:	eye, fig. true understanding, symbolic (Rev 4.8)
Peritome:	circumcision, sign of consecration to God and Jewish identity, met. righteousness (Rom 2.29)
Phos:	light, met. God's truth and love, understanding, virtue (Latin: lux Heb: or) (Jn 8.12)
Pistis:	faith, belief, trust in God (Col 2.5)
Pleroma:	that which fills, fullness, fulfillment (Rom 13.10)
Pneuma:	breath, wind, spirit, Holy Spirit, Heb: kodesho ruach, Pneuma Hagion: Holy Spirit (Lk 4.14)
Psiche:	breath of life, undying soul, life, emotions, appetite, Latin: anima (breath), animus (soul); Heb: nefesh (Ps 23.3)
Rhiomai:	deliver, rescue from (Is 59.20 Sept. rhiomenos deliverer) Heb: go'el redeemer (Mt 6.13)
Sarx:	flesh, body, human nature, carnal will vs spiritual direction from God (Rom 7.25)
Semeron:	today, this day (Mt 6.11 & Lk 2.11)
Sineidesis:	conscience, soul distinguishing between good and bad (Acts 23.1)

Soma: body, fig. the mystical body of Christ being the Church (Rom 7.24) (1 Cor 6.19)

Sophia: wisdom, Lat. sapientia Heb. chokma (Pro 24.3)

Splagchnizomai: have compassion, moved to the bowels (Heb. racham) seat of compassion (Mk 1.41)

Thelema: will, wishes, purpose of God to bless humanity through Christ (Mt 6.10 & Jn 6.38)

Theos: God, the creator and sustainer of all things, Heb. Elohim and Jehovah (Mk 12.29 & Lk 3.6)

Tiphlos: blind, orig. meaning darkened by smoke, used as a met. for spiritual ignorance (Mk 10.49)

Zoe: life, met. true faith and heaven, Heb. chayyim mayim hidatos zontos living water (Gen 26.19)

Author's profits from this publication, if there are any, to support the development of Franciscan Brother and Sister congregations and associations within the Protestant and Orthodox traditions, in particular reaching out in support for the Russian Orthodox Church Outside Russia (in Asia and Japan).

Profile

Stean Anthony

I'm British, based in Japan. I've written a series of books of poetry promoting understanding and peace. Find out more from the list at the end of this book. I have also published *Eco-Friendly Japan*, Eihosha, Tokyo (2008). *Monday Songs 1-5,* and *Eitanka 1* (pdf file textbook freely available on website – and sound files). Thanks to Yamaguchi HT for kind help.

New Projects
Great China 4 (classical Chinese poetry in English)
Saint Matthew 365 (verse-songs in Japanese)
Soulsongs (poems for peace in Jerusalem)
Saint Mary 365 Book 3 (verses for the BVM)
Monday Songs 6 (songs in English for study)

Prayer

Brightest power of goodness
Greatest light of eternal love
Grant that we may love one another more
That we may accept and forgive each other
That we may work together to make life
Better for all people
To lift up the children to better life,
Amen.

Word of Blessing

A blessing of peace
Be with us
And between us
In the spirit of love
People of every faith.

In all things
Thanks be to God
Amen.

Books by Stean Anthony with Yamaguchi Shoten
Original poetry & translations & adaptations. *Great China 1 & 2 & 3* (translations of classical Chinese poetry), *Kŏngzĭ 136* (poems based on the sayings of Confucius), *Songs 365* (poems based on the Psalms of David), *Songs for Islam* (poems based on verses in the Koran), *Sufisongs* (poems for peace in Jerusalem), *Inorijuzu* (Buddhist & Christian words for peace), *One Hundred Poems* (poems based on the Japanese classical anthology 百人一首 *Hyakunin Isshu*), *Manyōshū 365* (translations of ancient Japanese poems), *Saint Paul 200* (poetic phrases from the *Letters of Paul*), *Gospel 365* (based on the Synoptic Gospels), *Saint John 550* (poetic version of Gospel of St John for singing), *Isaiah Isaiah Bright Voice* (poems inspired by the Book of Isaiah), *Saint Mary 100* (poems dedicated to St Mary), *Saint Mary 365 Book 1 & 2* (calendar of poems on themes relating to Mary, Holy Mother, flowers, icons, prayer, scripture) *Selections from Shakespeare,* vols. *1 – 5* (passages selected from Shakespeare). *Messages to My Mother 1 – 7, Mozzicone 1 & 2*, essays & poems about questions of faith & other things. *Pashsongs* (poems by Stean Anthony, some reprinted & some new). *Monday Songs 1 - 5* (pdf textbooks of English songs). *Hagios Paulos 1* (narrative poem for singing). *Eitanka 1* (pdf textbook). "Psalms in English" (pdf 40 lectures on the Psalms).

MTMM series
HAGIOS PAULOS   Book 2
by Stean Anthony

Company : Yamaguchi Shoten
Address : 72 Tsukuda-cho, Ichijoji
          Sakyo-ku, Kyoto, 606-8175
          Japan
Tel. 075-781-6121
Fax. 075-705-2003
URL : http://www.yamaguchi-shoten.co.jp
E-mail : yamakyoto-606@jade.dti.ne.jp

MTMM series
HAGIOS PAULOS   Book 2   定価 本体1000円（税別）

2013年11月20日 初 版   著 者 Stean Anthony
                               発行者 山 口 冠 弥
                               印刷所 大村印刷株式会社
                               発行所 株式会社 山口書店
           〒606-8175京都市左京区一乗寺築田町72
           TEL：075-781-6121   FAX：075-705-2003
           出張所電話
              東京03-5690-0051   中部058-275-4024
              福岡092-713-8575

ISBN 978-4-8411-0919-1 C1182
©2013 Stean Anthony